# Vertigo to Go

Vertigo to Go

# Vertigo to Go

Brendon Booth-Jones

First published 2020 by The Hedgehog Poetry Press

Published in the UK by
The Hedgehog Poetry Press
Coppack House, 5
Churchill Avenue
Clevedon
BS21 6QW

www.hedgehogpress.co.uk

ISBN: 978-1-913499-25-9

9 8 7 6 5 4 3 2 1

A CIP Catalogue record for this book is available from the British Library.

Printed and bound by TJ Books Limited

For my sister, my best friend, Mix.

And in loving memory of Stella, Anthony and George.

# Contents

## I: **Whippet**

Ashley ............................................................................. 11

Testimony ........................................................................ 12

Dreamscape (Ash Awakes) .................................................. 14

Ritual ............................................................................. 15

Codex ............................................................................. 16

## II: **Vertigo**

To my crush who lives on the second floor ............................ 21

Chez toi ou chez moi ........................................................ 22

Poem for Elvis Schmoulianoff ............................................ 23

West Meadow .................................................................. 24

Autumn in Amsterdam ...................................................... 25

## III: **Tremor**

Kite ............................................................................... 29

Poem Scraped from Greasy Menu ....................................... 30

Catacombs ...................................................................... 33

I Don't Give a Fuck about Bach .......................................... 34

## IV: **Scythe**

Red Gavel ........................................................................................ 39

Ice Berg .......................................................................................... 40

Toothbrush ...................................................................................... 42

Sun on Stone on Sky ....................................................................... 43

Community ...................................................................................... 44

Hypnagogic Lyric ........................................................................... 45

Self-portrait in Dilated Pupil ......................................................... 46

Sonnet ............................................................................................. 47

Pain Braid ....................................................................................... 48

## V: **Patina**

January 1st, 3AM ............................................................................ 51

Market Research ............................................................................. 52

Anthology ....................................................................................... 53

Visitation ........................................................................................ 54

At the site of the crash ................................................................... 56

Poem for my Mother ...................................................................... 58

# 1: Whippet

*Ashley*

our 15 year old hands
cut it from a plastic Coke bottle
spray-painted it blue and fitted it with tinfoil

we named our homemade bong *Pandora*

thick white smoke straight into our blood

in Ashley's garage on Saturday nights
feeling like suburban teenage soothsayers
we grooved to Hendrix       we raged to Cobain
then we laid back on neon beanbags and
    the space between
          each thought
               stretched out like cosmic toffee—
and with blood-struck eyes we gazed
through dust-addicted cobwebs
      ragged and abandoned in the rafters
to the luminous tantalizing future
pinned like a shiny silver ring
          to the nipple of the world

but I grew up and fled that two-stroke town
lost touch with that boy and that vision
of a world without injustice

and now I wonder *Where is Ash?*
I asked around       tried to find a contact number
or Facebook account       but all I found:
another memory long buried
in pubescent wreckage of ecstasy
Purple Haze       Ninja Turtles and bad grades
      memory       rising like a pimple
    small and painful
of his voice in that damp garage saying
*Since my dad died I feel I'm breaking apart. . .*

and I had been too busy riding the radiant final wave
of innocence behind my eyes
          to see his hands shaking—

11

# Testimony

—For Sam Catsburg

rain-soaked Sunday night
in the chrome-gleaming megachurch—
the preacher preened in his cream suit

in strobe light and smoke he televangelized
at the red sea of dazed white faces:
his congregation:
absorbed bored scared or sincere

14 years old          bashful as Bambi
I sulked down the aisle
towards the refuge of the bathroom
and exited the shrieking preacher's packed auditorium

then I padded through the dark and empty
middle stanza
and as I pushed open the door to the WC
I heard a scuffle and turned
towards the green-lit emergency exit

where I saw a purple-suited preacher
throw a bearded and bedraggled
long-haired homeless man out
who might have hobbled in
to seek the blood of Christ        or simply
to escape the deluge of winter night

*Piece of heathen trash*        the preacher spat
slamming the door in disgust
before turning and locking his eyes on me:

*Ashley Bruce-Jane        I know who your stepfather is*
threatened the white-haired red-faced man
when he saw that I was frozen in the doorway
of a paradigm shift        my hands trembling
blush spreading over me like wine on a white dress—

12

it was one of those moments
when you either scuttle back
into the warm fold of all you've known

or you turn your back and leap into a dark future—

away from the sickly sweet cologne
of toilet freshener cloying your throat:
that synthetic smell of fake flowers
trying to cover shit—

## Dreamscape (Ash Awakes)

I step out of a trance        moonlight
fills the room to brimming
the weed has worn off        my brain is porridge
the garage smells of bongs and vomit

you're asleep        but your eyelids flutter
scanning a shifting dream vista:
you        me        Jimi Hendrix
        making frozen yogurt snow angels again?

molecules of memory
gather like blood to a bruise

I see my dad's face        his eyes closed
in rapture        playing me his Woodstock records—

to shake the pain I look at you
snoring lightly on a beanbag cushion
nails painted black        SpongeBob t-shirt—

do you feel this tension between us?

how soft are your moonlit features
        delicate as moth wings        you tease
you confuse        there is a tiny fold of skin
across each eyelid
where faint red lightning
        strikes the sealed horizon
                of your unfathomable life—

## Ritual

*—For Michelle*

Hymn books held our innocence intact: a pine-scented summer camp bible story glow. Until the acid drop, mic drop, starlessness and X. And we shredded the hymns to bits. Which seemed like some sort of rite or MTV ritual. But without the peroxided 90s angst our damage lacked disaffected heroin-chic Beckingham Palace tabloid glamour. It's true: nobody likes you when you're twenty three. *Not even you.* And the paper cuts! Guilt that sliced our fingers and eyes, our tongues and throats, our speech—and we covered our wounds and fear with masks of swagger. While miles away, microplastics clogged the lungs, hacked the liver of the ancient graceful whale navigating the lonesome Southern Ocean with her prehistoric celestial radar, her ancestors murmuring darkly in her huge, grieving, barnacled heart: *My child my child beware beware be*—at the house party, we plunged into the Gatorade-blue infinity pool on the long street of identical McMansions. Just like in the movies. Your teeth were pill-white, my frantic smile as wide as Buddha on speed—but later that night, even three Valiums deep, the chlorine-blue chemical sleep couldn't keep the big whale's frightened wheezing out of my dreams—

## Codex

*—For Toni B.*

the phone call that strips
the skin off the heart
the total pain that repaints
        every room in the body
the religion: a cardboard cutout of love
the school: a conveyor belt of hate
the stepfather's words:
        *Your daddy never loved you!*

the running away      the finding of friends
the floating in suspended fields
        of shimmering psychedelics—
the candy-flipping astral projections
        superimposing your DNA
           onto the dilated stars—

      but

the vibrant internal mandala     dissolving
the cold concrete cracked sidewalk of summer's end and

the poison coming back stronger:
        *Your daddy never loved you!*
        *You were a disappointment to him!*
       *I'll hit you to Heaven before you go to Hell!*

      and so

the slamming of the door forever
       Wretched King:     adieu!
the fleeing: this time you and your mother:
       her apologizing all
the way
    into
       single parenthood and then
the graduation     then
the taking flight
the losing of the self in
the world's bitter codex of questions:
the fear and vertigo and glitter—

# II: Vertigo

## To my crush who lives on the second floor

*—For Beatrice*

*Ghostfires from heaven's far verges faint illume*
—James Joyce

We met randomly in the elevator. Such a cliché. You dropped your keys between my feet. Occasionally we'd meet in the lobby and I'd try to convey my inner universe through my small talk. Once we met in the courtyard, where you offered me a Marlboro Red. *I quit years ago, but fuck it,* I never said. Instead I just said, *Sure.* Though you make me feel very *unsure,* in a thrilling, dizzying way, my heart rasping like a dragonfly against the window of your mystery. You use your cigarettes to flourish, to punctuate your sentences. You talk about computational biology and structural genomics the way most people talk about their favourite (endorphin flavoured) Netflix show. You're casually multilingual. You're a queer anime steampunk mystic with an IQ north of 150. You're so hard to read. That Sunday in the park when we went skating and I fell on my ass and afterwards we lay on the grass and ate ice cream and beyond the darkening trees the sky was fading into twilight's frail translucence and beyond the park the world was falling apart, and you kissed me and then said you preferred long distance dating—what did you mean? Is there some ecstatic purity in being denied? Are you a pierced and tattooed monk in disguise? Your enigmatic opacity, nimbly dipping and swerving out of reach (did I mention you're a rollerblade virtuoso?) made my sincerity feel like a clumsy puppy gambolling at your feet. But behind my cheerful folksy openness, aren't I really just as evasive? Aren't I also hiding all my fears, bewitched but ham-fisted, maladroit, with less feng shui than you? It's ridiculous to admit, but I started smoking again in the hope I'll bump into you in the courtyard. Most times, it doesn't happen, and I just stand beneath your lighted window, envying the ascetic unadorned walls that get to hold you in their gauche embrace! But I'm trying not to look in case you're looking down at me, but I'm always hoping you are, but you're probably deconstructing microbes for fun, and I stand in the dark courtyard, smoking till my lungs hex me, my blood turns to tar, and I look up beyond the top of our building at the faint, illuming, unreachable stars—

## Chez toi ou chez moi

—*For Jamie & Noémie*

Saturday night winter wine bar clamour
          laced with body heat
pouting lips     flustered faces     clinking glass
      dissolving inhibitions—

outside for a smoke I saw the full moon
      frozen in a pale radiance
                  ancient and undiminished

by the city below
      the semi-real neon bee hive
heaving through its speed-blur of consumption—

back inside         over the tang of sweat
    over the wild slosh
            of haute couture slur     sensuous selfies
        fashion faces     flushed money
              parting lips     crescendo laughter
        I heard the words:
                  *Your place or mine?*

22

*Poem for Elvis Schmoulianoff*

sky of smudged thumbprints

bone-white snowdrift in slow mo

flame-blue hair electric in the lamplight

angelic lashes glimmer black

hieroglyphs of smoke in the lamplight

dark rainbows in her laughter lines

faux-leather boots to crush fascists

wine-dark trench coat flowing

time gathers in the gutters

time holds its breath

o anime moth

you circle upward

in the spindrift of snow

falling silver through the night

falling falling falling

like a million white petals or

like shredded hymns into the street

## West Meadow

—*For Ella*

at a barf-worthy party      trying to avoid
those who put the *harm* in *charm*
          we found each other
that night had seemed destined
to drag like bad acid
     but you turned it like a volta

you led me by your silken perfume compass
     and half a bottle of flat champagne
away from the seasick slurring
         ferris wheel of fun

to the fragrant emptiness of the West Meadow

where you graced the star-silvered heather
     and my eyes
       with your presence

but     finally alone
without the fuzzy crutch of drunken hubbub
our chromosomes twisted our tongues in knots

my lips issued one misprint after a mother

at the peak of my awkwardness
not knowing what to do with my hands
         I high-fived a nearby rosebush—

and your laugh was a glittering rivulet
and you kissed my dough-damp hand
and our energy shimmered and rippled
and we danced beneath the genderless stars
      that swayed like drunk angels
        over the moon-washed midnight meadow—

## Autumn in Amsterdam

*—For Daniëlle & Sharelle*

we picnic near the pond in Vondelpark
the light does its best impressionist impression
day saunters into dusk
ducks dab for morsels in the soup-thick water
your feet curl up behind you
and to the sole of one shoe is stuck
a grey plug of gum jeweled
with a little rusted fishing hook
and a tiny reel of hair—
as if the world were trying to hook you
to stop you floating away forever
down the burning river of sky draining gold in the west
and I lay there beside you thinking up
these ridiculous lines          and others
that I will never publish
such as how your eyes sparkle like endorphins
and your lips gleam like dolphins          and so on
while you fumble with an outrageously expensive kiwifruit
and I visit each island in the archipelago
          of freckles on your arm with a kiss—
now the evening air is perfumed with dew
and the dank stink of weed
and tourists tumble bug-eyed through golden leaves
but nature senses a coming death
and summer is a husk
among the empty cans and pizza crusts
so why can we never return
to the freshness of unknowing?
the North Sea breathes her fishy frigid breath
another season of excess moulds in the rubble
and this scene will soon be drained of colour
so come closer and let's push
the end of the poem back
          a little further—

# III: Tremor

*There is in God, some say,*

*A deep but dazzling darkness*

—Henry Vaughan

## Kite

*—For Pauline & Tim*

Ash     it's me     Mom
my Ash          where are you
I was unpacking the boxes
in my new council flat when I found
a patch of that red material
your father used to build kites
when you were little     my Ash
remember the red kite
how you flew it together
you and your beloved father
on the dazzling white sand     my Ash
how you ran squealing with delight
along the shore beneath the pale blue sky
of your childhood now I count the years
in the spots of mould mapping the ragged
red flags of memory I haven't heard
from you in months my Ash please call me

## Poem Scraped from Greasy Menu

*—For Gio & Julz*

You might ignore me
when I bring the menu over
in this faux-rustic franchise café.
(The vintage pictures are mass-printed,
      the flowers are fake,
           the scuffs in the wooden tables
are well placed, the ambience hand-picked
    from a catalogue of great taste).
You might snap your ringed fingers with impatience,
bark your order for the Salmon Bagel Sensation,
talk loudly on your iPhone 21, plunder
the Amazon, Earth's left lung—
yes, I heard the words, saw the oil glow black
on the lips you lick, heard you preen over
your hostile takeovers, automated abattoirs,
dollar-green gleam in your eyes—
How dare you tear this planet to shreds!
(And how I make myself sick with acquiescence,
                  hoping for a tip).

But here's a knife and some salt,
here, sir, is the scoop:
beneath the façade
of wholesome home cooking heaves
the vast godless operation:
the sleepwalk of flex-work drudgery:
the dishwasher thumbing your cutlery,
the herniated cook dropping your bagel
cream cheese-side-down
        on the sticky kitchen floor,
and yes: the barista
burning your double espresso into
        a carcinogenic brew—

And that salmon, sir, was dyed pink and pumped
with preservatives. Slave-wage workers
with weeping minds picked your precious coffee beans—

But the planet you tamed climbs back up the chain
in blind revenge. No apex predator escapes.
Earth rolls back red eyes (red claws, red fangs).
Don't you see the blazing December sun? The snowy summers?
The ocean up to its throat in microplastics?

Buried under the waxen grin of nip, tuck and botox
is a shrivelled man, and buried under him
is a young child who loved dinosaurs, bees and flowers,
the dappled sunlight through the trees,
the snug winking of the lighthouse in winter.

So how did you make that leap
from carefree to cruelty?
Are you a shark blossoming
from the rich landed slaver soil
so neatly sealed
beneath the lush green garden
where you were planted?
And what does that make me?
Periwinkle, plankton, peasant?

But how to hate you when you sit here
looking like my neighbour's pitiful pet
puffer fish named J. K. Rolling,
king of your plastic pirate ship
so cutely adorning your tank,
when in truth you're power-hungry, money-flushed,
you fuss with your Gucci collar,
finger the keys to your Ferrari, leave no tip,
drive your children's children to their graves.

And then I look across the café
and out at the lunch-hour city,
suited and booted bustle
of brick, bicycles, bagels and canals
and the rapid clouds' hustle
churning and lurching over Amsterdam,
late for their next big contract with the sky.
And a ginger cat on a low brick wall
across the street
stands still, one paw raised, waiting—

## Catacombs

*—For Ben Rodgers*

The weather was demure and mild,
Paris in summer is pretty as the flowers
in the Jardin des Plantes—

But I couldn't get it right.
I walked too fast. I walked too slow.
I chewed too loud. I mumbled.

I hesitated and we missed the metro,
and had to wait an extra seven minutes
in the piss-reeking passages, stepping
over the blistered feet of homeless people
slumped against the grimy white tiles.

I lost our tickets to the Louvre. I didn't listen.
I forgot the charger in the Airbnb. *I'm sorry*
*but that simply isn't good enough.*

So why put yourself through such torture
in this gritty, resplendent place,
this paradoxical tome
of refugees and retro chic,
guillotines and grand romance?

Why not ditch me at the border to your heart,
instead of leading me into its catacombs!
And what does my willingness to enter that labyrinth
say about me? And what does my willingness
to write such a petulant poem say about me?
Maybe we're perfect for each other, after all.

But now that I'm in these tunnels, we're in trouble.
I take the wrong route, I get us lost, skulls loom
like resentments. I fumble with the map.
You snatch it from me and storm off in search of an exit.

## I Don't Give a Fuck about Bach

*—For Pam*

I finished unpacking the last of my stuff,
the Amsterdam sunset a pink smudge
outside my window.
I decided to put on some iTunes Bach—
Italian Concerto in F Major—
and let the majestic stream rush through me
on Ad-Free settings—

When I opened my eyes I saw the bottle
of Jack Daniels on the bookshelf
between *The Tempest* and *The Beach*
with the handwritten note still looped round the neck
saying, *Sorry for your loss—*

I took a big gulp and only then,
as the sweet dusty fire touched my tongue
and throat and belly,
did I notice the fat dead fly
drifting near the bottom of the bottle.
*This is not a symbol,* I told myself, nervously.
*No dead planet drowned in man-made amber poison—*

And then I heard a knock at the door,
then a pounding like a war drum
or raving psytrance song
polluting Bach's soaring magnificence—

I opened up
and my new neighbor, burly and blonde,
all jaw, pectoral and faux-tribal tattoo—
like a muscle-wrapped package
of masculine insecurity
delivered to my door,
with chlorine-blue eyes, told me,
*Turn that shit off I'm trying to sleep.*

*What, that music?* I croaked,
throat suddenly dry as a week-old McNugget.
*But—but that's Bach's Italian Concerto in F Major!*

And he blinked once,
as if I'd addressed him in Swahili,
and then he pointed a finger
the colour of uncooked sausage
at my face and said,
*You're about to have a "major" problem.*
*Because I don't give a fuck about buck.*

# IV: Scythe

*a lethal light I orbit the depths,*

*my blind fishes and I.*

—Isabelle Kenyon

*Red Gavel*

—*For Curtis*

beneath the surface of our small talk whisper aquifers of why

above the paint-brushed river
            the frozen explosions of high winter cloud

under these clean sheets are the stains of past loves

behind the symmetry of your smile        a deeper sadness

pain & joy on one side        indifference on the other

above the cars like beetles gleaming over the bridge
                        alarming news headlines

over the planet fumes unrelenting
frenzied weather      at both poles
                            icebergs splitting up
            icebergs without alimony &
                    the mercury's red gavel rising

beneath the how's your new job        the *why am I so alone*—

## Ice Berg

—*For Sierra*

I limped away from you
along the motorway
and crossed the bridge over the Amstel River.
Fenced in by winter's black corrugated iron trees,
the city was a cemetery of high-rise headstones.

These backwater outskirts of Amsterdam
ached beneath a sky grey and bright
as bones under X-ray.

Ants held an orgy in a rotten half rat
half squished into the print of a bicycle track.
Trucks thundered past like elephants on meth.

And my tendons were taut from the stress of our syntax.
After we'd carved our tongues into daggers
I cut up the tea-cosy of your confidence
and you stabbed me in the leg of my hope.

I stopped and stepped up
to peer over the rail, as if looking out
over the murky, tweed-brown sheen of my life.
*Close my eyes and my head starts spinning.*
*Keep them open keep them—*

And down below me on the river
drifted a long steel barge
like an oil-smudged and armour-plated iceberg,
carrying huge yellow mounds of sand—
                              enough to fake a beach.

And isn't that how we lost our way,
drifting further and further from home, looking
downstream over each other's shoulders to the next
tantalizing bend, hoarding idealistic piles
of dirty blonde hope
for a better life in some unknown harbour?

Seagulls bickered overhead over bread.
The black latticework of forest stood unmoved.
Then the blue howl of a police siren
rinsed through me like detergent.
I slowly raised my hands

to wave the industrial barge
and the bitter grit of its burden goodbye
as it passed under the bridge
on its course to someone else's horizon.

*Toothbrush*

—*For Sona*

At the bottom of my old dank toiletry bag
I found your blue toothbrush,
crusted with greyish,
vaguely minty-smelling toothpaste,
and a thick springy pubic hair—
      like a quiet bolt of black lightning—
caught in the worn and splayed bristles.

And for a fang-sharp minute
you were here again,
with the bed sheet creases
imprinted on your morning face,
your faint smell of nameless flowers,
and a frothy white grin as you brushed your teeth
and told me of your day's plans,
stacked with fakery
on the verge of unraveling—

I stood there gripping the toothbrush,
gripping an old pain
I thought I'd recycled,
but had merely washed down
to the blotched and forgotten
toiletry-bag-bottom of memory.

Then the fridge hiccupped. The image shattered
easily as a promise,
and the silence closed round me again like a forest.

And then I flung that poison arrow straight in the trash.

But we all know plastic lasts forever—

## Sun on Stone on Sky

*—For Jonesy*

the sun is given an injection of romance in its fiery spine
the valance of cloud is embossed with gold
      over the mountains which are a statue of you
lying supine across my horizon
cold stone eternal art installation
couldn't we avoid
another hyperbolic heartbreak poem? why
must night always fall
into old habits? the strung-out city's neon throb
like a cheap imitation of stars
miles from here but still
leaking meaning into the desert
the moon rouged crudely in the day's dust
rises to wrap up the present tense—
ready for the night shift

## Community

—For Fritz

Ash. It's me. Your unnamed narrator.
I have some questions.

Have you made it this far?
Have you ever wondered
about you and me, what we might have been?
Have you ever had the feeling
        of nostalgia for someone else's life?

What right do I claim
to repaint my own pain
into the shadow of your shape?

Please forgive my crude musings.

But everywhere I turn I think I catch a glimpse of you.

Was it you who flashed past me
in the souped-up gleaming black Mercedes,
death metal snarling at full volume
behind windows black as the toenails
of the other you

I saw last night, asleep on the steps
in front of the supermarket.
One stray shopping trolley
abandoned by the flock
shivered in the deserted parking lot.
One flawed, distraught, beautiful person
falling through this loveless version
of *community*. Ash. Was that you?

*Hypnagogic Lyric*

—*For Kings & Joy*

I couldn't sleep     a motorbike
ripped the throat out of the silence
down the dark street below my window

I pulled back the curtain
and looked for the moon
but there was no moon in this poem

I couldn't sleep I wrote this
poem in Morse code
I listened to Sparklehorse
I did a Sporkle quiz:
          a Multi-Category Minefield Blitz

I looked at the cables of vein in my wrists
and felt heart-sick with longing for you

a car door slammed somewhere in the night

trucks hummed far off on the highway

I closed my eyes
and my ex-stepfather's stern finger loomed accusingly—
then loosened and curled into a white-maned wave:
the last page of a chapter: I saw again my mom
packing the car us leaving him gasping in the driveway
him shrinking forever in the review mirror

I heard a beating of wings and a whoosh:
I opened my eyes
and saw my blue-haired Muse
on her chariot of bats
          float through the wall towards me
in slow motion                    like a ghost ship
          semitransparent—
eyes hearse-black     sword drawn
     baring her fangs—
                         *Pandora is that you—*

45

## Self-portrait in Dilated Pupil

—For Evrim & Marv

day after day of skittery sleeplessness
If I stopped straining for God's garbled whispers
could I learn to be fluent in whale-speak

the sunlight might wreck itself in the glass vase
the festering reptile of my flaws might be vanquished
but here I am with my dedication to distraction
and here they are with their shiny algorithms

have you ever abandoned ship
these days for a fiver you can lick your own endorphins
        in any given nightclub toilet for a year-long minute
what would dad think of me now
strobe light and bass in my bones        vertigo-to-go
        with each sip we bottle the sparkle in our eyes
and then we exit night's nostril and scatter
                our youth into the umpteenth dawn

do you remember
that long winter when I painted
        self-portraits
in the liquid black of your pupils

sometimes his voice would open like a chrysalis
but flit so fast into the moth-eaten edge of memory

now mostly what I sense when I see his smile
is a remote sadness        sepia fading into snow

but maybe it's the lack of sleep that gets me
days strung together like fake pearls

## Sonnet

Breaking news: the news is broken. Purpose is replaced by a plastic replica. How fast does my attention fade on a scale from Brexit to breakneck? Cute Cat Singing Christmas Carols! From gaol he escapeth and flourisheth! Battery acid, drain cleaner, lantern fuel and antifreeze. Our Father who art in Heaven, on the count of three say *Cheese.* This Rubik's Cube is for J-Wow & Lee. This content isn't available right now. Methylphenidate, magnesium stearate, polyethylene! E453. Covid-19. Buy these dreams to take the edge off! But I've only got one left? Multiplexed hybridization leading to high throughput spectrometry. Duh! Find a hot date in your area tonight! Jejune spoonerism. Obamarama. Insert subtext here. Add a liberal twist of olive oil and lemon. Jesus wept. Jesus wheels. There is a quasi-polynomial time approximation algorithm achieving mad street cred. Yet another species is dead. Hey you at the summit of this toxic system! Doesn't the vertigo make you sick? Or is power your medicine? 404 page not found. Can't we grind to powder the structures upon which we hang our High Street hunger? McMonster. McMafia. McWorld. How dare you sell our future to (y)ourselves! And all the while the snails still trace their ancient script of mystic glitter on dead leaves in damp fields. And tonight the moon is our housebroken stone—O pale-faced pup! The poet's faithful pet on a leash of allusion. *And who's a good dog? Who's a cute moon?*

## Pain Braid

*—For Al & Manuel*

Number of times you washed your hands today: 27—
Knuckles rubbed raw as skinned rabbits. Time
holds another hymn
of microplastic up to the light. Every
bagel is a Morse code
concerto. Dolphins
tumble bug-eyed through
the dark and empty middle codex—

Did you feel that? *Feel what?* Exactly.
　　　The hearse-black volta of syntax.
　　　　　My child, my child. Beware!

*I can't go on*　　　　no it's fine
　　　　it's fine　　　　Valium

*Your daddy never loved you.* Stop.

　　　　So sorry for your loss　　　of plot

and something rolls
　　back its eyes and　　draws
　　　its fangs　　　claws up
　　all the memories
　　　　you own and
　　spits them against
　　　the bathroom mirror
　　　　in which I stand blinking

*daddy loved you very much Ash he's gone he's gone daddy's gone*

48

# V: Patina

# January 1st, 3AM

*—For Dad*

groggy from bong hits—no more
wasting time on petty self-needling—no more
no more standing lonely in the kitchen
            eating pasta from the pot
                        for a hug of carbohydrates
radiant ferris wheel of amphetamines—never ever again
no mask no casket no fake flowers of half-hearted sparkling—nope
no dope swizz pingers or disco biscuits
no stocks or shares in falling foes
no stacking it down the stairs of friendship
no hiding behind newsfeeds and digital thrills
no more wallowing in wounds and bruises
less popes more poems
always more poems
more yes more hope more looking up
more reason to call myself your son—

## Market Research

—*For James Mone*

& running late for my stodgy job
at the crumb-smudged call centre
in the drizzling city
brown brick        brackish harbour smells
slaver statues & high street chains in the rain
fast food chains      ciggie butts      spires
dead wet leaves spinning dizzily
over my skull-drill hangover
so late I couldn't even stop
to take the stone out of my shoe
but realised then and there
wince by wince
that I should probably do something
about the stone
made of fangs & curses
invisible & massive
blood diamond
anchored in my chest—
thinking always what works for me is best
my unforgiveness my addictions my regret
my desire to be anywhere else than here—
& all of it satin-wrapped in a quilt of privilege—
to be safe in my white skin        to not deal daily
with the gun-cold shoulder of living history
and what to do about this self-inflicted
perpetual lateness to get a grip
        of time ringing like a phone
                in an empty room—

## Anthology

—For the Writer's Block Magazine board

then gradually
granularly
to find your creaking way
to the holy anthology
of art activism therapy friends
and to be
washed
in a waterfall
of solace and music

to revisit
the dizzy heights
and the muddy gutters
still shakes you—

but hey      at least
you no longer stagger
in the neon-green
and tiger-striped
strobe of your panic—

in typical fashion
the pyrotechnic shiver
becomes a flicker

but the migraine in your heart
is reconfigured

*ragged psyche*      *meet sublimation*

# Visitation

—*For Tim Seng Ong & Seb Harris*

It was a Wednesday night in Amsterdam. One A.M. April's green buds tangled into May. Spring's first follicles emerging. Late capitalism pulling its million sugary triggers. In the air, fragrance of flowers and pollutants. On the bike ride home from my lover's house my ecstatic woe was suddenly ruptured. An ancestor awoke inside me and looked out at the cold, quiet, starless city. He didn't take possession: it was more like we shared my vision, tucked snugly inside evolution's billion-stanza poem (also known as my standard edition human brain). We sat side by side, looking out of the sad sleepless portals of my eyes. And I whispered to this Neanderthal being (forgive me if I misplaced his eon) as much explanation as I could muster (signifier after signifier) of this glossy, digitized, terrifying version of the world. 'Look,' I said, 'at the shining city lights dancing on the dark canals, the manicured feng shui gardens fringed with cherry blossom and wisteria, the stone horses frozen to the pedestals of Western history, and this billboard obsession with being young forever. And how good we are at collective forgetting! This glittering wealth was paved with blood.' My friend said, *Duskwéntowrdhos ?esti?* But I speak neither Elvish nor Proto-Indo European. So I said, 'Ice cream, cinema, wireless, streaming, H.D., global travel, high speed, literacy.' And we peddled on through the deserted streets, passing now the business district, office lights burning in empty cubicles.

Just then, a sleek Mercedes rolled into the illuminated McDonald's drive thru, smoother than a bird of prey across a plain—'But the real birds gag on plastic, the plain is peeled for profit, and Earth tosses nightly in a fever dream. Animal rights, human rights, free speech, blood transfusion, antiretroviral, open heart surgery, penicillin, and still we will not let people love who they choose and who they choose to be, still we build abattoirs, live in the lie of whiteness, kill each other over what to believe.' I could feel my friend's coarse beard and deerskin shawl prickle the inside of my face as he twisted in the cave of my head to better catch the looping nasal language of the future, smoke signals murmuring from the first fire. 'And in my pocket I have a thing of similar size to one of your crude tools, and within it I have access to the mind of history—or at least several versions of it. Yet all I do is try to scroll the loneliness away—while faceless corporations push species after species down the ravenous black hole of extinction.'

My companion gave one great sob, and then he was gone, and I missed my chance to tell him of poems that melt weapons into saxophones and imagination and hope—did he dissolve back into my bloodstream to stay submerged another hundred thousand years? Maybe he seeped through my pores and drifted away into the crisp night air, up towards the tusk of crescent moon, that ever present relic, half buried this utterly still night in a mammoth of cloud.

* Duskwéntowṛdhos ʔesti *means 'The omen is bad' in Proto-Indo European, the hypothetical language from which most European languages are said to have descended.*

*At the site of the crash*

all is thunderingly still.

The street, trees and houses
lie curled asleep in the predawn chill.

Silence hangs heavy as extinction.

But one truck wheel still spins.

We are first on the scene.

The truck must have swerved to dodge
a cat, caught the curb at high speed and flipped
in slow motion

to crunch and buckle upside down into the stop sign
and then the wall of the dentist's office,
telephone wires smoking and tangled like a toxic jellyfish.

Hands shaking, you rush back to the car
and call 911.

I am frozen before the wreckage.

Somebody's son somebody's somebody—

Blood coats the steering wheel, blood on the bible, blood
on history, a man scythed by the half-sunk sickle of his belt—

a body wracked by impact and glass.
He is dead. He is dead.

How thin is this veil of living! These lamp-lit
quiet suburban streets
stretched like frail skin over
the swirling sewers of darkness. Oh stop
turning this into a poem. Stop turning. Please make this stop.

Stop the birds' incandescent songs of waking.

Stop the dawn shaking rose-fresh petals of exquisite red skyward.

Stop the first morning walkers who gather to gawk.

Finally, a siren fills the air with its screech.

Somebody's son, brother, father, lover—
                    split apart and wasted.

From eye to synapse to psyche,
the image is coded into language.

From paper to pixel to data, dissolved
in the digital bloodstream and forgotten—

except by the vast unconscious:

the shock of the blooming red skull,
the face a crumpled page emptied of narrative—

and, dangling from the cracked dashboard,
the blood splattered picture of a little boy.

## Poem for my Mother

Mom      you are the kindest person I know
kind and gentle yet so damn brave—
it was you who taught me
that there is a point in the Pacific Ocean
where the water is so clear
and so deep
that you get vertigo
just from looking down
when you snorkel on the surface
gazing down through
the blue gradations
aquamarine
emerald
indigo
shadow steeping
beyond the silver glint of fish
and the angel wings of manta rays
down into
the impenetrable depths
miles below
dark as the ink of amnesia—
and you taught me not to look away—

*Vertigo to Go* offers a fast-paced and arresting snapshot of adolescence, exploding at the same time any comfortably nostalgic remembrance of a youth culture haunted by a deluge of microplastics and escalating species extinction. Booth-Jones skilfully combines humour with a genuine sense of pathos about the current environmental crisis and multinational capitalism.
—Dr. Emelia Quinn, Co-editor of *Thinking Veganism in Literature and Culture*

*Vertigo To Go* is a tender and intimate, but also visceral and thought-provoking, testament to Booth-Jones' exquisite ability take us on a journey of growth and reflection. It will force you to confront parallels in your own lives, may even floor you with emotions you had not expected to feel, but will definitely leave you satisfied at the end.
—Dr. Cyren Wong, Founder of NatureTalksBack

The stage set in *Vertigo to Go* is NOW but the song is a timeless one. I hear my own voice in every line.
—Charlie Calder-Potts, creator of *Singing Some Endless Song*

*Acknowledgments*

Thank you to the following journals for publishing some of these poems in earlier forms (and sometimes with different titles):

*Anti-Heroin Chic:* 'Self-portrait in Dilated Pupil'.
*The Blue Nib:* 'Hypnagogic Lyric' and 'At the site of the crash'.
*Botsotso:* 'Dreamscape', 'Codex' and '*Chez toi ou chez moi*'.
*Fly on the Wall:* 'Poem Scraped from Greasy Menu'
*Ghost City Press:* 'Ritual'.
*Peeking Cat:* 'Sun on Stone on Sky'
*Scarlet Leaf Review:* 'Ashley', 'Autumn in Amsterdam', 'I Don't Give a Fuck About Bach', and    'Toothbrush'.
*Writer's Block Magazine:* 'West Meadow', 'Sonnet' and 'Anthology'.

Thank you to the English Department of the University of Amsterdam.

Thank you to the tireless and big-hearted champion of contemporary poetry, Mark Davidson, the man behind Hedgehog Poetry Press. Thank you for believing in my work.

Thank you to my family, friends, artists and teachers for all your love and inspiration.

*Duskwéntowrdhos ʔesti* is borrowed from
https://ceisiwrserith.com/ritual/practice/adfrituals/ritualphrases.htm

Epigraphs come from:

'The Night' by Henry Vaughan (public domain)
*This is not a Spectacle* by Isabelle Kenyon (with the author's permission)

Cover photo by Brendon Booth-Jones

## About the Author

Brendon Booth-Jones is the Editor-in-Chief of *Writer's Block Magazine* at the University of Amsterdam. Brendon's photographs, poems and prose have appeared in *Anti-Heroin Chic, Amaryllis, As It Ought To Be, Botsotso, The Blue Nib, The Bosphorus Review, Fly on the Wall, Ghost City Review, The Night Heron Barks, Odd Magazine, Otherwise Engaged, Peeking Cat, Scarlet Leaf Review, Zigzag* and elsewhere. *Vertigo to Go* won the 2019 White Label Trois Competition.

Find him on Facebook @brendonboothjoneswriter and Twitter @BrendonBoothJo1

Photograph with cat © Ella King.
Author photograph © Jill Pellikaan.
Cover and all other photographs © Brendon Booth-Jones